This

Was Written

completed

For

JASON

By

AVERY

so don't worry!!! i have endless like for you.

I LOVE YOU DAD!!! ...

→ and I also like you.

• As much love as there tends to be in families, there isn't always as much like.

EYP Publishing
www.eyppublishing.com

ISBN: 9781077300200

This is so cheesy with the hands...

Thank You For Being

So incredibly giving.

I could never express how lucky I feel because of that.

a child of that age could never complete this book.

I
Learned
How To

EX: ↙ <u>Appreciate</u> ¿ <u>Try</u> ↘

cars
songs
EX:
people
<u>to do the right</u>
movies
<u>thing</u>
words
<u>to be the best</u>
funny things
<u>person I can</u>
good inventions
<u>be. really.</u>
old houses
<u>in school,</u>
random idioms/phrases
<u>sports, etc.</u>
the sky
<u>to create</u>
treefrogs
<u>happiness</u>
good yards
<u>when I've</u>
neat grass
<u>lost it</u>
porches
<u>to do</u>
efficiency
<u>things well</u>
<u>the first</u>
<u>time</u>

By
Watching
You

One of My Favorite Things About You Is How You

_____

When You

_____

The Song That Reminds Me Most of You Is

_____

_____

One of My Favorite Times Is When I Get To
_____
With You

Your Hidden Talent Is

_____

_____

I Smile When You

I Really
Enjoy

_____

_____

With You

You
Are
Really
Good
At

_____

_____

You Changed My Opinion About

_____

_____

The Movie About Your Life Would Be Titled

_____

_____

Everyone Should

_____

_____

Like
You Do

You Are Really Good At

_____

_____

_____

I
Am
_____

About

Your
_____

You
Make Me
Better At

_____

_____

I
Need
Your

_____

_____

I
Am

About
Your

I
Love
Going To

_____

_____

With
You

You
Make Me

When You

I
Love To

_____

_____

With You

I Am Surprised At How Much I Enjoy

With You

The Next Time We Decide To

_____ ,

We Should

_____

You

Make

The Best

The Three Words That Describe You Best Are:

_____,

_____,

and

_____.

You
Inspire
Me To

_____

_____

I Love
How
You
Believe In

_____

_____

The Way You Makes Me

One of My Favorite Times Is When I Get To _____ _____ With You

I Will Never Grow Tired of Your

_____

_____

You
Are The
Most
Amazing

_____

_____

Ever

One of My Favorite Times Was When We

_____

_____

Never

Stop

The Way

You

_____

_____

Your

Makes

Me

If

Were Muscles, You Would Be the Strongest Person in the World

You
Are
Perfect At

_____

_____

My Favorite Thing You Cook Is

_____

_____

Thank You For Helping Me

_____

_____

There is
No One
In the
World
Who Can

Like You Do

I Always Appreciate It When You

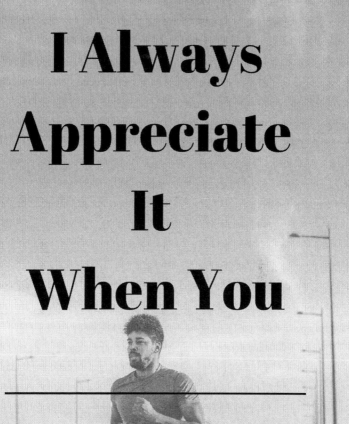

If I

Had

One Wish,

I

Would

Wish

For You

Your
Super
Power
Is

_____

_____

You Always Make Me Feel

_____

_____

I Love
To
Hear
Your
Stories About

_____

_____

The
Best Advice
You Ever
Gave Me Was

_____

_____

The Question I Have Always Wanted to Ask You Is

_____

_____

Dozens of Years From Now, I Will Still Want Your

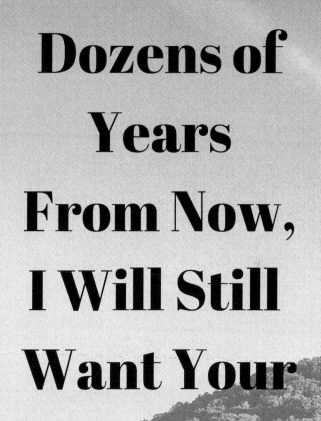

One

Day

I Want

To

_____

Just

Like You

You Are

The

Most

_____

_____

In The

World

I Always Laugh When You

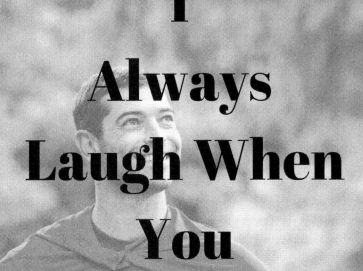

_____

_____

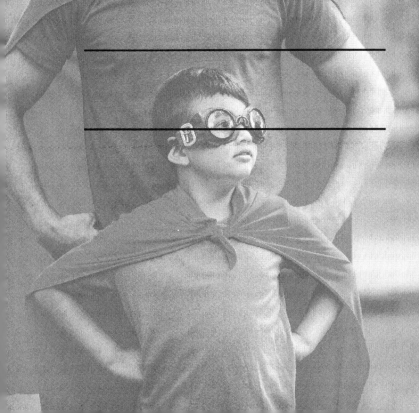

The Word I Would Use To Describe You Is

JASON

That was truly the word I felt captured as many parts of you as possible ↑

Seems random but I thought about it a lot ↑

Just kidding, I thought it'd be funny to be incredibly literal and put your name. Real word = effective.

I
Love
How
You Always
Encourage
Me To

_____

_____

You Should Get An Award For

_____

Well Done

The Way You

Makes Me Want to Cheer

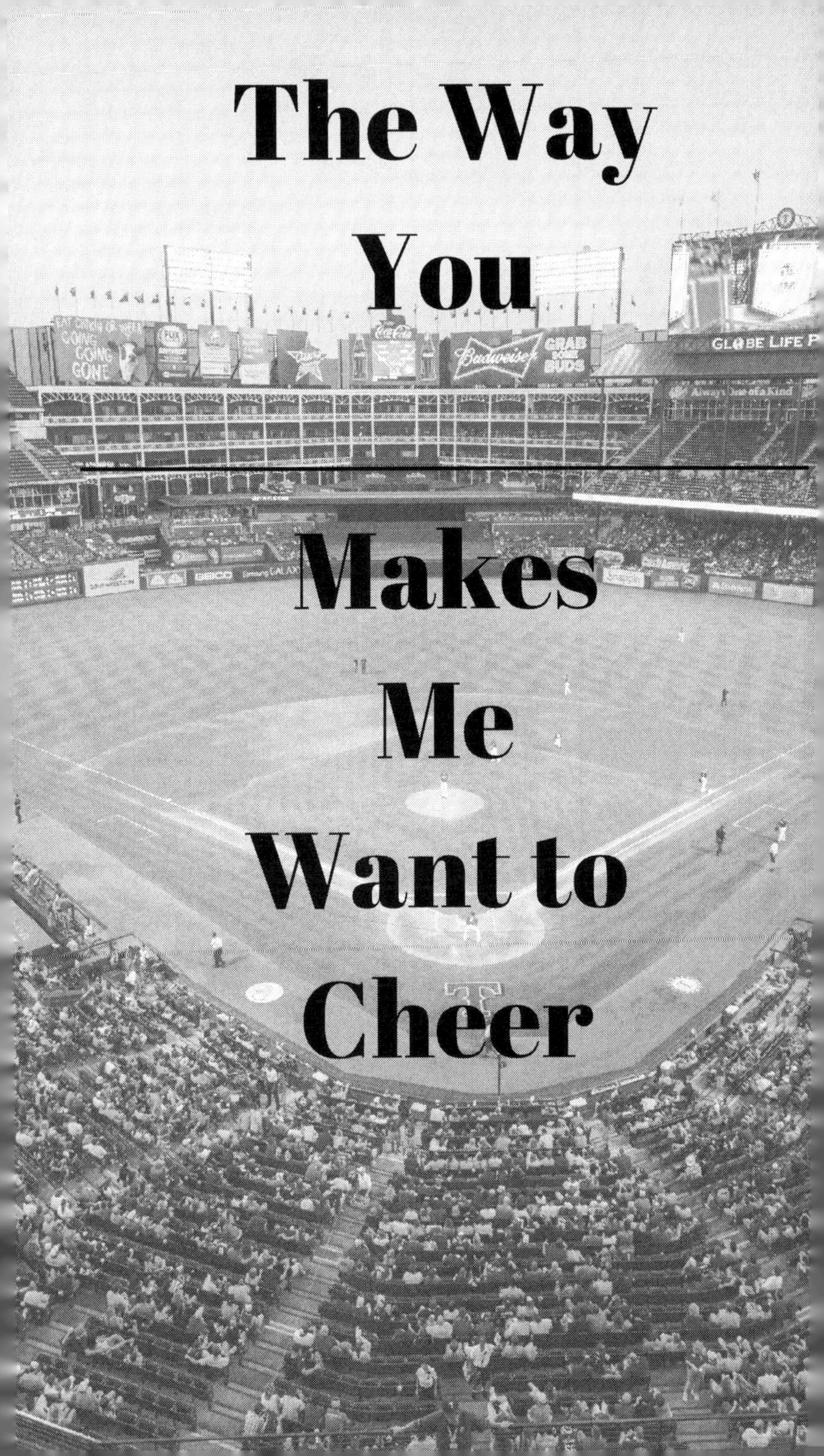

Thank You For How You

_____

_____

You Make Me Feel Special When You

share my excitement

with me—whether

in school, sports,

interests, or just

something happening

in my life

We Should Take A Trip To

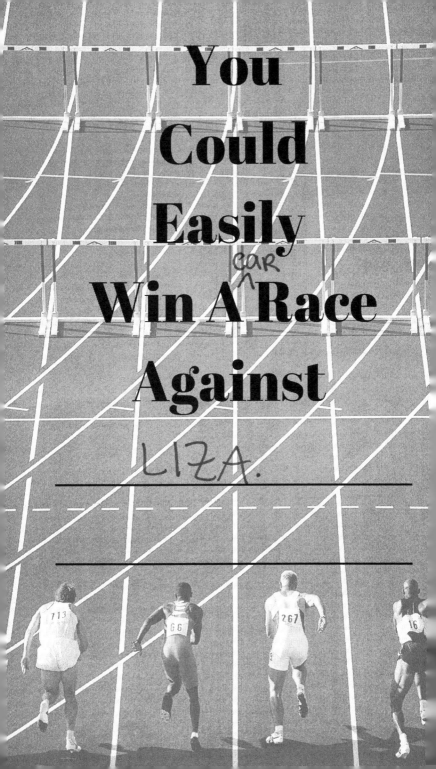

You Could Easily Win A ^car Race Against

LIZA.

_____

_____

I
Will
Forever

Hope to give my

kids as amazing

and fortunate and
encouraging and
valuable of a life
as you've given me.

You can reach us at
www.eyppublishing.com

Our fun, and
thoughtful creations
are available on
Amazon at

www.amazon.com/author/eyppublishing

EYP Publishing creates tools for people to share their stories, express themselves, and declare their dreams.

EYP stands for "Expand Your Parameters" and we want people everywhere to move beyond their comfort zones, believe in possibility, and live the life they were meant to live and have the relationships they deserve.

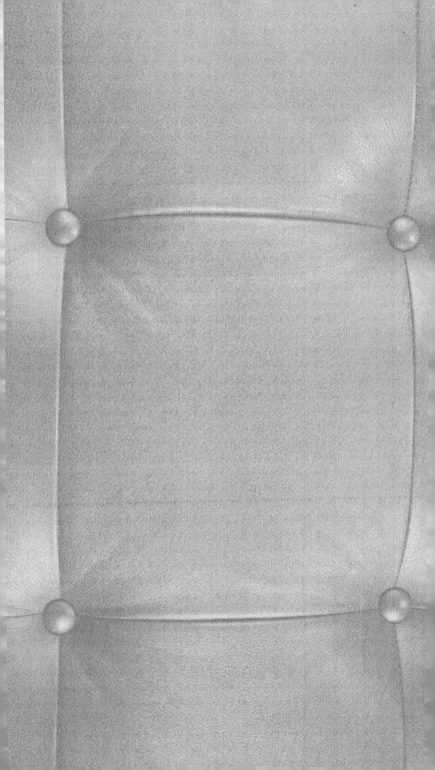

Made in the USA
Columbia, SC
12 February 2020